The Comeback Blessing

When God Restores What Life Has Broken

Copyright © 2025 by Mary E. Winfrey

All rights reserved. No part of this book may be reproduced, stored in a retrieval system, distributed, or transmitted in any form or by any means, including electronic, mechanical, photocopying, recording, or otherwise, without prior written permission from the publisher, except in the case of brief quotations used in reviews or articles.

Published by Alegna Media Publishing
United States of America

Cover design & Interior layout by
Alegna Media Publishing

All Scriptures quoted in this book are from the King James Version of the Bible unless otherwise noted.

This book is an inspirational work of nonfiction. Some names and identifying details have been changed to protect the privacy of individuals. Any resemblance to actual persons, living or deceased, is coincidental and unintentional.

For permission requests, inquiries, or bulk purchases,

Email:

The Take Over Academy

Email: info@takeovercoachingacademy.com

ISBN: 979-8-218-89707-9

Printed in the United States of America

Table of Contents

About the Author	*iv*
Acknowledgments	*vi*
Introduction	7
The Eden Complex	15
Grave Clothes Don't Look Good on You	25
Spiritual Freeloaders and Seed Droppers	44
Toxic Connections	54
Don't Call Me Naomi	65
Pressed But Not Crushed	84
God's Restoration Plan	100
Treasures, Not Trash	115
It's a New Dawn	126
A Call To The Kings	133
The Epilogue	139

ABOUT THE AUTHOR

Apostle Mary E Winfrey is a woman after God's own heart whose life stands as a profound testimony of faith, endurance, and divine restoration.

As the visionary founder of Faith Deliverance International World Ministries and Safe Haven Transitional Inc., she has devoted her calling to equipping leaders, nurturing spiritual growth, providing services for the wounded and abused, and guiding individuals towards healing and renewal. Through her ministry, she helps others rediscover the beauty of God's promises, even in the midst of life's most challenging seasons.

Apostle Winfrey firmly believes that there is a blessing in the pressing and continually exhorts believers to persevere in faith, pressing towards the promises of God, where desire meets divine purpose.

Through her own journey, she has come to understand that every trial carries within it a divine purpose and that God indeed gives double for your trouble. Her ministry is marked by an unwavering passion to see lives transformed through the hope, prayer, and power of God's Word.

Apostle Winfrey resides in Georgia with her loving husband, children, grandchildren, and great-grandchildren - each a reminder of God's faithfulness through every generation.

Apostle Winfrey continues to serve faithfully, inspiring countless others to walk boldly in their God-given calling and to trust in His unfailing promise of restoration and double blessings.

ACKNOWLEDGEMENTS

Space prevents me from acknowledging all those who have been an inspiration and influence in my life, but please know that I will never forget you. Thank you for being a valuable part of my journey.

First and foremost, I give honor and praise to Almighty God, the Father, the Son, and the Holy Spirit, who has kept me through every challenge, growing pain, and various seasons of life.

To my husband Vincent, my steadfast companion who has prayed with me and for me, faithfully standing and remaining by my side through every season of this journey.

I also want to thank our children- Monique, a pastor whom God is using in extraordinary ways as He manifests His gifts through her life; and our son, Michael, a strong leader whose influence continues to grow as he excels in his work and builds his own business. Thank you both for your unwavering love, patience, and encouragement. Your belief in me has been both my strength and my anchor.

I honor the memory of my late mother, Bishop H.D. Hamilton, now resting in glory, whose life was a living testimony of what God can do and how He can use anyone for His glory. Her faith and resilience continue to guide me. She often reminded me to stay in the race, never to throw in the towel, but to continue on course and endure to the end. She spoke words that still resonate deeply: "You have a story to tell, people to reach, and through God, the power to change lives with your testimony." Today, I stand upon her shoulders with unconditional love and reverence, determined to extend the work of God's Kingdom beyond the boundaries she once faced.

I express my sincere appreciation to my spiritual leaders, mentors, and all who have poured into my life, recognizing and nurturing the callings and gifts that God has placed within me. Through their prayers, instructions, and guidance, many of the messages that God entrusted to me have been preserved and, now in His appointed time, are being released for His glory. I'm so thankful for the encouragement that has been both prophetic and pivotal.

Twenty-eight years ago, it was discerned that there were powerful books within me waiting to be written.

To each of you, thank you. Your faith, support, and love have helped shape the vessel I have become.

Introduction

Somebody reading this book is tired.

Tired of waking up to the same pain that put you to sleep last night. Tired of wearing a smile like it's a uniform while your soul is screaming. Tired of being the strong one, the together one, the "blessed and highly favored" one when inside you feel like you're falling apart in high definition, a disaster that nobody else can see. Let's be real, unhealed wounds shape everything.

They shape the way you love, the way you trust, the way you show up in relationships, even the way you see God. You can only hide the pain for so long before it leaks out in your words, your choices, and your silence.

That's why so many of us walk around smiling while silently bleeding. We're singing or preaching in church, but broken inside. We're taking care of everybody else while secretly feeling stuck in the grave clothes of disappointment, rejection, and neglect.

If we're truly honest, some of us are just tired. Tired of coping. Tired of pretending. Tired of waiting for "time" to heal us, only to realize time doesn't heal; only God does. And until we deal with what broke us, we can't step into what God has prepared for us.

Unhealed pain has a way of sneaking into every part of our lives. It keeps us replaying old conversations, stuck in cycles of rejection. It makes us settle for "seed droppers" and "freeloaders," people who take but never invest. It convinces us that we'll never be whole, never be enough, never be loved. But do you know that the devil is a bold LIAR?

Broken is not what God has designed for your life. Psalms 34:18 *The Lord is nigh unto them that are of a broken heart and saveth such as be of a contrite spirit. (KJV)*

This means that God is near even in times of pain, trauma, and brokenness. Listen, when this verse speaks about a broken heart, it's talking about real pain. The kind of emotional pain that has you on your knees at 2 AM. The "contrite spirit" refers to a heart that's been humbled and has stopped trying to fix itself. A heart that's finally ready to say, "God, I need you."

Let me tell you something: feeling broken isn't a weakness. Do you hear me? It's not weakness. It's actually proof that you know there's something more than this mess you're in. It's evidence that your spirit recognizes you were made for more than grave clothes and disappointment. We, believers, need to understand that when we hit rock bottom, when we're at our lowest point, when we can't even lift our heads, that's exactly where God meets us. Right there in the pit. Right there in the pain.

This verse is a promise. It's telling you to cry out to Him with whatever voice you have left, even if it's just a whisper, even if it's just "help." Because He is Jehovah Rapha, the God who heals. He can heal you in every place that you hurt. Not just your physical ailments, but he can and will heal your mental and emotional pain as well. He's simply been waiting for you to stop pretending you've got it all together and just let Him be God in your broken places.

It is not by accident that you hold this book in your hands. Whether you purchased it or it was gifted to you, it is purposeful. You're supposed to have it because you need it. There is brokenness, pain, or trauma that needs to be healed within you, or perhaps within a loved one. Whatever the case, this book will be your roadmap from brokenness to wholeness. It brings together two powerful sermons that I preached several years ago.

How Bad Do You Want It? The challenge to shake off the past, break the chains, and decide you won't live in defeat another day.

Seasons of Refreshing -The reminder that God hasn't forgotten you, that your due season is still ahead, and that you still qualify for the blessings of God.

Together, they carry one mission: to help you rise from the ashes of yesterday and step into the fruitfulness of tomorrow.

See, we've been taught that "time heals all wounds," but that's not true at all. We've been told to just "let go and let God," but nobody tells you what to do when your hands keep reaching back for what hurt you.

As I preached in these messages:

"Hurts, humiliations, horrors from past relationships are the kind of memories that need to be healed."

"Painful memories can lie hidden from conscious thought, while draining large quantities of spiritual and emotional energy."

"A victim mentality is when you let your past dominate your present, which in turn blocks your future."

Let me be crystal clear: this book is not for people who want to stay broken. This book is for you if:

You're ready to say, "I must leave where I am to get where I want to go."

You believe "It's up to you to change your situation."

You're ready to break the chains and free yourself

If anything, that you have read so far has resonated with you, then this book is for you. I need you to know something right now, before you read another word, before you turn to another page. Your brokenness has an expiration date. And that date is closer than you think.

My question to you is, *how bad do you want it?*

Bad enough to let go of what hurt you?
Bad enough to take off your grave clothes?
Bad enough to believe God still has a season of refreshing with your name on it?

If your answer is "yes," then get ready to turn the page, but before you do. I want to say a prayer over you.

Lord, somebody picked up this book in their winter season, but they're about to walk into their spring. Somebody started this introduction wearing grave clothes, but they're about to experience a wardrobe change. "Give them the courage to say, like Tamar, 'I must gather my strength and move forward, for I have a purpose to fulfill.' Instill in them the faith to rise, like Naomi, when she heard that You had provided for her people. "For the one who's been wounded and broken-hearted, heal them right now. Let this book be their season of refreshing, their new dawn, their breakthrough moment. Heal the places time could not reach. Restore the hope life tried to steal. Let every page be a step toward wholeness, freedom, and fruitfulness.

In Jesus' name, Amen.

Now turn the page and prepare to exchange your grave clothes for glory!

Chapter 1

The Eden Complex

James Brown wrote a song in the 1960s titled "This is a Man's World." It rang out like a bold statement of how men have dominated in technology, business, and progress. But he didn't stop there, he turned the corner and reminded us, *"But it wouldn't be nothing, nothing without a woman or a girl."* In other words, men may build, create, and conquer, but it is the presence of a woman that gives life meaning, purpose, and completion. Without her, the world is empty.

While I understand the meaning of the song, my perspective takes it deeper. Oh, I certainly agree that men need women. They may be the head, but the women are the necks that turn the head! We could laugh and jester on that topic all day long, but the truth of the matter is that we actually need each other.

At the end of the song, the lyrics show how men can feel emotionally distant and bitter. Even though they've built and achieved a lot, they often end up feeling alone in the world they created. This highlights how complex and challenging gender roles and expectations can be. We put a lot of weight on each other when we aren't able to handle it. That's why we see so many people depressed, acting out in anger, full of anxiety, and oftentimes suicidal. It's all because we are carrying burdens that we weren't meant to carry.

Here is where my perspective takes things deeper. It may be a man's world, but it's nothing without God in it. God is the one who gave man dominion over the earth to replenish, create, and multiply, but we all know how that story ended.

Listen, before the fall, we had a perfect place on this earth. Paradise wasn't some fairy tale or metaphor. It was real, it was here, and now it's gone.

Eve, whom I call the mother of discontent, had been blessed with every perfection by God. Not some perfection, not most perfection, but every perfection. She had a constant companion in Adam, someone who would never leave her or forsake, never ghost her, never make her wonder where she stood. Her body was free of sickness and disease. No cancer scares, no chronic pain, no mysterious symptoms that doctors couldn't diagnose. She had the perfect diet, everything fresh, everything pure, everything exactly what her body needed. She did not need to hide behind masks or filters, no fear keeping her up at night, no need to control or manipulate, no battles to fight. All she and Adam had to do was receive all the good God was pouring out.

But Eve made a choice. She decided to eat the fruit by accepting the serpent's insinuation that God was withholding something from her. One conversation with a serpent, and she bought the lie that the Creator of the universe was keeping the good stuff for Himself. And just like that, the perfect love that had permeated every molecule of that garden no longer existed. It didn't fade away gradually. It was there one moment, gone the next. Adam and Eve discovered what every person who's ever made a deal with the devil discovers: they traded priceless treasures for empty promises.

Genesis tells us that when God created Adam and Eve, He gave them more than just breath in their lungs and food to eat. He gave them Himself. "And the Lord God planted a garden eastward in Eden; and there he put the man whom he had formed" (Genesis 2:8). Eden wasn't just a garden. It was the place where heaven and earth touched, where God walked with man in the cool of the day. Adam and Eve had intimacy with their Creator, a life free from shame, and a love that required no performance. They had wholeness.

They lost the perfect fellowship they once had with God. They were cast out of Eden, away from the tree of life, and forced to live in a world where pain, toil, and death would become part of their reality.

From that day forward, humanity has been living with the ache of Eden's loss. Every generation since Adam and Eve has carried that homesickness for what was lost. It shows up in the way we chase after things, hoping they'll make us whole. Some of us try to fill the void with success, while others seek fulfillment through relationships, money, or recognition. Some try to drown the ache in addictions or distractions. But no matter how much we strive, the emptiness remains because what was lost was not a thing. It was a relationship.

The Eden Complex is not just about missing a garden; it's about missing God's presence as He designed it from the beginning. Ecclesiastes 3:11 says, "He hath set eternity in the hearts of men." That means no matter how far we wander, there is something inside of us that remembers. Our souls know there's more, and that longing will never be satisfied with anything less than Him.

Think about Adam and Eve after they left the garden. They carried the memory of what it felt like to walk in perfect harmony with God. Imagine how heavy that must have been to remember the sound of His footsteps in the garden and know they would never hear it the same way again. We carry that same memory in our DNA. We weren't made for brokenness. We weren't designed for shame. That's why betrayal cuts so deep, why loneliness feels so crushing, and why grief can hollow us out. We live in a world that has lost its original design, and our souls know it.

The problem is that most of us spend our lives trying to medicate that ache instead of addressing it. Just like Adam and Eve reached for fig leaves to cover their shame, we reach for temporary fixes to cover our wounds. We hide behind busyness, behind status, behind carefully curated lives that look whole but are still fractured inside. But no fig leaf can replace the covering of God's glory. No achievement or relationship can substitute for His presence.

Deep down, we're all longing for a place we've never seen, a home our hearts remember but our feet have never touched. We're all chasing relief for an ache we can't seem to soothe, reaching for fixes that never satisfy. What we're really feeling is the echo of Eden's loss, and no number of substitutes will heal it. Only God, the One we were made for, holds the cure our souls crave. In other words, we are all broken and only God can heal us.

Human beings need to love, be loved, and believe that we are significant. These aren't wants; they are needs. Just like your body needs air, water, and food, your spirit needs love, connection, and purpose. But because of the fall, because of that failed perfection in Eden, we're trying to meet those needs in all the wrong ways.

Some of you are trying to earn your wholeness. You're on every committee, at every service, volunteering for everything, thinking that if you do enough, you'll feel complete. But you're exhausted and empty.

Many of you are trying to buy your wholeness. New car, new house, and new clothes. thinking that if you just have enough, you'll feel complete. But you're in debt and still desperate.

Others of you are trying to relationship your way to wholeness. Jumping from person to person, heart to heart, bed to bed, thinking if you find the right one, you'll feel complete. But you're more broken with each goodbye.

Romans 8:22 reminds us, "For we know that the whole creation groaneth and travaileth in pain together until now." The whole world is groaning for restoration, waiting for God to make things right again. That groan is the Eden Complex. It's the restless cry of humanity for a wholeness we can't manufacture on our own.

But here's the good news: what was lost in Eden is restored in Christ. Jesus came not just to forgive sin but to reconcile us back to God. Paul writes in 2 Corinthians 5:18, "And all things are of God, who hath reconciled us to himself by Jesus Christ." In other words, Jesus came to bridge the gap, to lead us back into fellowship with the Father. The cross was the doorway back into what was lost.

Yet even as believers, we can still struggle with the Eden Complex if we don't allow Christ to heal our broken places. We can be saved and still restless, forgiven but not free, in church every Sunday, but still longing for more. Why? Because wholeness isn't automatic. It takes surrender. It takes allowing God to touch the places we've hidden, the wounds we've tried to cover, the pain we've carried so long that we've convinced ourselves it's just part of who we are.

The Eden Complex is God's reminder that you were made for more. That emptiness you feel is not a curse; it's a compass. It points you back to Him. It's God whispering, "There is more than this. Come closer."

You are not crazy for feeling like something is missing. You are not weak for aching for more. You are human, made in the image of God, longing for the wholeness that only He can restore. And the truth is this: you don't have to stay broken. Just as God walked with Adam in the garden, He desires to walk with you now.

So the question becomes, how bad do you want it? How willing are you to lay down the fig leaves and reach for His covering? Because the same God who banished Adam and Eve from Eden is the same God who sent Jesus to bring us back into His presence. He has made a way for the ache to be healed, for the void to be filled, for the Eden Complex to finally meet its cure.

Chapter 2

Grave Clothes Don't Look Good on You

There's something about grave clothes that nobody talks about. They're comfortable. Not comfortable in a good way, but comfortable in that familiar, broken-in way. You know what I'm talking about. It's comfortable like that old, worn gown or that raggedy pair of shoes that you should have thrown away years ago. However, because they are so comfortable, you tend to hang on to them. That shame you've been carrying for ten years now fits you like a glove.

That rejection you experienced has become part of your identity. That hurt has become your uniform, and you've gotten so used to wearing it that you've forgotten it was meant for dead people, not living ones.

Pain has a way of clinging to you like a second skin. Shame wraps itself around your spirit and convinces you that you are what you've been through. Disappointment sits on your shoulders until you get so used to the weight that you forget it was never meant to be carried. Those are grave clothes. They are the garments of death, meant to bury what has no life.

Let me tell you about a woman named Tamar who wore grave clothes for years. Not by choice, but by circumstance. Not because she wanted to, but because life dressed her in them, and she didn't know she had the power to take them off.

Tamar's story is found in Genesis 38, and if you've never read it, buckle up because this isn't your typical Sunday school story. This is raw, real, and relevant to every person who's ever been dressed in disappointment and told to wear it like it's normal. Her story provides a vivid picture of what it's like to live bound and how dangerous it can be to remain that way.

Tamar was a Canaanite woman who wasn't supposed to be blessed. She came from the wrong side of the tracks, the wrong bloodline, the wrong everything according to society's standards. But by God's grace and mercy, she married into the family of Judah, one of the sons of Jacob. She married into the blessing.

Her first husband was Er, whose name literally means "to be watchful, to look." Now pay attention to this because some of you are bound right now to an Er in your life. Er just sat back and watched. He stood around checking things out. The majority of his relationship with Tamar consisted of watching and receiving freebies. He was what today we call a freeloader, someone who takes and takes but never gives, never invests, never commits.

The Bible says Er was wicked in the sight of God, and the Lord slew him. Just like that, Tamar found herself wearing widow's clothes. First grave outfit. She didn't choose it. Life put it on her.

According to custom, she was given to Er's brother. His name means Onan, "strong" or "pain," and sadly, he embodied both. On the outside, he had strength, but his choices left behind only pain. He was strong enough to take what he wanted from Tamar, but he wasn't committed enough to give her what she needed. When the time came to honor his duty, to give her children, to secure her future, to carry on his brother's name, he deliberately spilled his seed on the ground.

That made him what I call a seed-dropper. He was present for the pleasure but absent for the purpose. He wanted intimacy without investment, access without accountability, benefits without responsibility. Seed-droppers are dangerous because they look like they are participating, but they never intend to produce. They take up space, they consume energy, but when it's time for commitment, they pull back.

We see this same spirit at work today. Some people will connect with you for what you can give them, but when it comes time to build, grow, and plant something lasting, they vanish. They want the thrill of being connected to your anointing, your talent, your vision, but they don't want the weight of responsibility that comes with it. They enjoy the benefits of the relationship, but they drop the seed when it's time to carry the load.

The story goes on to tell us that God killed him too. Second grave outfit. Another layer of loss for Tamar; another garment of grief.

Then Judah, her father-in-law, told Tamar to go back to her father's house and wait. Wait for his youngest son Shelah to grow up. Wait for another chance. Wait for the promise to be fulfilled. And Tamar waited. And waited. And waited.

The Bible says, "Tamar put on grave clothes, a type of widowhood." These grave clothes were symbolic of disappointment, hurt, abuse, something that all of us have experienced at one time or another. She wore them for years. Years of waiting for a promise that was never going to be kept. Years of hoping for a future that was never going to come. Years of being bound by someone else's broken word.

Some of you are wearing the same outfit right now. You're dressed in the disappointment of broken promises. Wrapped in the rejection of relationships that didn't work out. Covered in the shame of mistakes you made or mistakes that were made against you.

Grave clothes can look like fear that paralyzes us from moving forward. They can look like unhealthy relationships that we cling to because we are afraid of being alone. They can look like addictions that numb our pain but never heal it. Grave clothes disguise themselves as comfort when in reality they are a coffin. And you've been wearing these grave clothes for so long that you've forgotten they're not your actual clothes. They're not who you are. They are just what life puts on you.

The enemy would love nothing more than for you to stay wrapped in what hurt you. Because as long as you are bound, you cannot bear fruit. As long as you are bound, you cannot fully walk in your purpose. Tamar's life looked like it was over, but she had to come to a place where she recognized the garments she wore were not her final destination.

Here's what keeps you bound: when you let your past dominate your present, which in turn blocks your future. That's what I call a victim mentality. It's when the grave clothes become so familiar that you start introducing yourself by your pain. "Hi, I'm divorced." "Hello, I'm a survivor of abuse." "Hey, I'm an addict." No, that's not who you are. That's what happened to you.

The blocks that keep us bound are hurts, pains, and spirits of offense that we hold on to. We clutch them like they're precious when really they're poisonous. We protect them like they're treasures when really they're trash.

Think about Tamar for a moment. She had every right to be bitter. She'd been given to two brothers who failed her. She'd been promised to a third who was withheld from her. She'd been sent back to her father's house like returned merchandise. She was wearing grave clothes that society said were appropriate for her situation.

But here's the thing about grave clothes: they're designed for people who aren't moving anymore. They're designed for people who have no future. They're designed for people whose story is over. And as long as you're wearing them, you're living like you're dead when God says you're alive.

Tamar reached a point where she decided enough was enough. She took off her widow's garments, her grave clothes, and positioned herself for something new. She made a decision that she would not die in disappointment. She would not live forever in rejection. She refused to let shame be her permanent address.

Now here's where Tamar's story gets interesting. Here's where it goes from tragedy to triumph, from victim to victor, from grave clothes to glory. The Bible says Tamar heard that her father-in-law, Judah, was going up to Timnath to his sheepshearers. His wife had died, he'd finished mourning, and he was moving on with his life.

And something shifted in Tamar. I believe she said to herself, "I must leave where I am to get where I want to go. I must come out of this grave of pity, hurt, despair, and feeling rejected, neglected, and forsaken. In other words, I must get myself together because I've got some place to go!

She decided to break free from the grave clothes that she'd worn for so long. Breaking free begins with a decision. You cannot change the past, but you can refuse to let it chain you to the ground. Jesus said in John 8:36, *"If the Son therefore shall make you free, ye shall be free indeed."* Freedom is already available, but you have to choose to walk in it.

Tamar took off her widow's garments. She took them off! Nobody did it for her. No prophet came and declared her free. No priest came and performed a ceremony. She made a decision that enough was enough, and she took off those grave clothes herself.

Are you tired of struggling? Do you want your life to change? Then understand this: IT'S UP TO YOU TO CHANGE YOUR SITUATION. Not your circumstances, but your situation. Your circumstances are what happened to you. Your situation is how you're responding to what happened to you. Paul wrote Philippians while in prison, yet he said, "I have learned, in whatsoever state I am, therewith to be content" (Philippians 4:11). His circumstances were imprisonment, but his situation, his mindset, and his response were peace and contentment.

Tamar couldn't change the fact that two husbands had died. She couldn't change the fact that Judah had lied to her. She couldn't change the past. But she could change her present response to her past pain. She could take off those grave clothes and put on something else.

Breaking the Chains That Bind

You must decide to break the chains and free yourself. How bad do you want it? Because if you want it bad enough, you'll stop protecting your pain like it's precious. If you want it bad enough, you'll stop rehearsing your hurt like it's a speech you have to give. If you want it bad enough, you'll stop wearing your wound like it's a medal of honor.

Let me tell you what Tamar did that was so revolutionary. She didn't just take off her grave clothes; she put on different clothes. She covered herself and positioned herself where Judah would see her. Now, I'm not advocating for deception here. I'm showing you the principle: she changed her position to change her provision. She moved from victim to strategist. She went from passive to active. She shifted from waiting for life to happen to making life happen.

And here's the key: she made sure she would be compensated. When Judah wanted to sleep with her, thinking she was a prostitute, she just didn't accept whatever he offered. She said, "Give me your signet, your cord, and your staff as a pledge." She got collateral. She protected herself. She ensured that this time, she wouldn't be used and discarded.

We need to get what I call the "whatever spirit." Whatever it takes to be free. Whatever it takes to break these chains. Whatever it takes to take off these grave clothes. Whatever fear I have to face in showing up differently. Whatever courage I need to muster to demand what I deserve. Whatever!

Some of you have been wearing grave clothes for so long that people identify you by them. They expect to see you defeated. They're comfortable with you broken. They've gotten used to you playing small. And when you take off those grave clothes, they're going to be uncomfortable. They're going to question you. They might even try to put them back on you.

But you have to develop a whatever spirit that says, "I don't care what you think. I don't care what you expect. I don't care what makes you uncomfortable. These grave clothes don't look good on me, and I'm taking them off."

Here's how Tamar's story ends, and this is the part that should make you shout: Tamar got double for her trouble. When Judah found out that the "prostitute" he'd slept with was actually his daughter-in-law Tamar, when she presented his pledges as proof, he said something remarkable: "She has been more righteous than I."

She didn't just get vindication; she got elevation. She didn't just get recognition; she got restoration. She gave birth to twins, Perez, and Zerah. Perez became the ancestor of King David and ultimately Jesus Christ. The woman in grave clothes became the woman in the bloodline of the Messiah. Out of her pain came purpose. Out of her rejection came restoration. Her story declares that grave clothes are temporary, but God's plan is eternal. The Canaanite who wasn't supposed to be blessed became the carrier of the ultimate blessing. Whew, that's a good place to shout if you ask me!

So how do you take off your grave clothes? Let me give you the practical steps:

How do you break free?

First, by naming what has bound you. Stop pretending it is not there. Call it out. Is it fear? Is it rejection? Is it trauma from your childhood? Is it shame from a decision you made years ago? What are you wearing that was meant for a dead version of you? What pain, shame, rejection, or failure have you wrapped yourself in? Name it. You can't remove what you won't acknowledge. The power of the grave clothes is broken when you shine light on it.

Second, make the decision. Nobody's coming to undress you. You have to decide that today is the day you stop dressing for a funeral when God has called you to a future.

Third, take action. Tamar just didn't think about taking off her widow's garments; she actually did it. What action do you need to take? Do you need to forgive someone? Do you need to leave a toxic situation? Do you need to seek help? Do you need to stop rehearsing your hurt? Whatever it is, do it.

Fourth, put on something different. Don't just take off the grave clothes and stand there naked and vulnerable. Put on praise. Put on purpose. Put on power. Put on the identity God says is yours. You are not what happened to you. You are who God says you are.

Fifth, position yourself differently. Tamar positioned herself where blessing could find her. Where do you need to reposition yourself? What rooms do you need to enter? What conversations do you need to have? What opportunities do you need to pursue?

Listen to me carefully: Those grave clothes don't look good on you. They never did. They are not your size because you were made for glory, not grief. You were designed for victory, not victimhood. You were created for purpose, not pain.

The same God who saw Tamar in her grave clothes sees you in yours. The same God who orchestrated her deliverance is working on yours. The same God who gave her double for her trouble has double waiting for you.

But you have to take off the grave clothes. You have to break free from what's binding you. You have to decide that you want wholeness more than you want sympathy, that you want freedom more than you want familiarity, that you want future more than you want to hold onto the past.

As we close this chapter, I want you to stand up right where you are. I'm serious. Stand up. Look down at yourself. What are you wearing spiritually? What grave clothes have you wrapped yourself in? What death garments have you been walking around in?

Now, make the motions of taking them off. Start with your hands and literally act like you're removing a coat, a shirt, pants, whatever. As you do, speak to those grave clothes:

"Rejection, I take you off. Shame, I remove you. Failure, you no longer fit me. Abuse, you're not my identity. Addiction, you're not my covering. Depression, you're not my outfit. Anxiety, you don't look good on me."

Keep going until you've named and removed every grave cloth you've been wearing. Then put on your new clothes:

"I put on righteousness. I put on peace. I put on joy. I put on purpose. I put on power. I put on love. I put on wholeness."

You might feel silly doing this, but remember Tamar. She had to physically take off those widow's garments. Sometimes spiritual freedom requires physical action. Sometimes, a breakthrough requires us to do something that feels uncomfortable, unusual, or even embarrassing.

How bad do you want it? Bad enough to take off what's familiar? Bad enough to remove what's comfortable? Bad enough to let go of what's been your identity for years?

Your double for your trouble is waiting. Your elevation after devastation is ready. Your restoration after desolation is prepared. But first, you have to take off those grave clothes, because, again, I say, "they don't look good on you."

Leave those grave clothes in this chapter. You won't be needing them where you're going.

Chapter 3

Spiritual Freeloaders and Seed Droppers

You just took off your grave clothes in the last chapter, but let me tell you something that might save your life: there are people waiting to put them back on you. There are folks who are invested in your brokenness, comfortable with your dysfunction, and threatened by your freedom. These are what I call spiritual freeloaders and seed droppers, and if you don't learn to recognize them, they'll keep you bound longer than any chain the enemy could ever forge.

See, the enemy is smart. He knows he can't always attack you directly. Sometimes you're too prayed up, too filled with the Word, too covered by the blood. So what does he do? He sends people. He sends relationships that look like blessings but function like curses. He sends connections that feel like comfort but operate like cages.

Tamar's story isn't just about grave clothes. It's about the people who kept putting them on her, the relationships that dressed her in death, the connections that confirmed her worst fears about herself. And until we understand how toxic connections keep us broken, we'll keep returning to the very people who help us stay bound.

The Er Spirit: Watchers Who Won't Work

Let's go back to Tamar's first husband, Er. His name means "to be watchful, to look," and that's all he did. He watched. He observed. He took notes, but he never contributed. He never invested. He never worked.

We have a lot of Er's in the church arena as well as in the world. They're watchers, spectators, not participants or workers. They won't get involved in anything. Won't join the choir, won't join the praise team, won't usher, won't do outreach, they won't even say amen, no matter how powerful the message is. They just sit back and watch.

But here's what makes them toxic: they're watching you. They are in *your* life, taking up space, consuming your energy, benefiting from your presence, but never pouring back into you. They're what we call freeloaders in our present day. They want all the benefits of a relationship without any responsibility.

Have a few people come to mind yet? You know who I'm talking about? That friend who only calls when they need something. That family member who shows up to all the dinners and never brings anything, but leaves with three plates. That romantic interest who wants all your attention but won't fully commit. That ministry partner who wants to share the spotlight but never wants to serve. The Er spirit is toxic because it makes you feel like you're in a relationship when you're really in a transaction. And the transaction is always one-sided. You give, they take. You pour, they receive. You invest, they withdraw. And the whole time, they're watching you exhaust yourself trying to make something work that was never designed to work.

Here's what spiritual freeloaders do to keep you in bondage: First, they drain your energy. Every relationship requires energy, but healthy relationships replenish what they take. Freeloaders just take and take until you have nothing left to give, and then they make you feel guilty for being empty. They'll say things like, "You've changed," or "You're not the same person I met," when really you're just exhausted from carrying the entire relationship on your back.

Second, they diminish your value. When you're constantly giving to someone who never reciprocates, you start to believe that's all you're worth. You begin to think that maybe you don't deserve someone who invests in you. Maybe you should be grateful for whatever crumbs of attention you can get. Maybe this is as good as it gets for someone like you.

Third, they occupy space that is meant for better. As long as a freeloader is in your life, taking up emotional real estate, there's no room for genuine connections. You're so busy trying to make a withdrawal from an empty account that you don't notice the people trying to make deposits into your life.

There's an old saying: "Why buy the cow when you can get the milk for free?" That's the freeloader's motto. They've figured out how to get all the benefits of your presence without any investment in a true relationship. And as long as you keep giving them free milk, they'll keep showing up with an empty bucket.

Er was wicked in the sight of God, and the Lord slew him. That should tell you something about how God feels about spiritual freeloaders. They're not just annoying; they're wicked. They're not just draining; they're dangerous.

When someone watches your life but won't contribute to it, when they observe your struggles but won't help carry your burdens, when they benefit from your growth but won't contribute to it, they're not just being lazy. They're being wicked. They're violating the very principle of love that says we should bear one another's burdens.

Don't link up with any Er's. For the men, don't be or become an Er. Don't be the person who watches life happen around you while contributing nothing. Don't be the spouse who expects to be served but never serves. Don't be the church member who critiques every service but never volunteers for anything. Don't be the friend who has opinions about everyone's life but no investment in anyone's growth.

The Onan Spirit: Present for Pleasure, Absent for Purpose

Let's talk about Tamar's second husband, Onan. His name means "strong" or "pain." Scripture tells us that Onan took his brother's widow, Tamar, as his wife. He went through the motions. He stood at the altar. He participated in the union. He embraced the benefits of having her as his wife. But when the moment came to fulfill his true responsibility, when it was time to give Tamar children to secure her future and carry on his brother's name, he refused. Instead of planting the seed of promise, he deliberately spilled it on the ground.

There are spiritual Onans sitting right in the pews. You see them on the usher board, the deacon board, singing on the praise team, clapping in the choir, or serving on a committee. They show up when the music is good, when the crowd is hyped, when the spotlight is shining, when it feels like a celebration. They are present for the excitement, but absent when the real work begins.

Because the moment accountability shows up, the moment sacrifice is required, the moment holiness is preached instead of hype, they drop the seed. You can preach prosperity, and they'll shout you down. You can preach name it and claim it and they'll dance in the aisles. But preach about presenting your body as a living sacrifice, preach about sanctification, preach about commitment, and suddenly the seed hits the ground. They check in for the performance but not for the purpose. They show up to be seen, not to be transformed.

Seed droppers are present for the pleasure, but absent for the purpose. They invest just enough to look committed, but never enough to carry the promise. They give the appearance of life but produce nothing lasting. Their pattern is predictable: they start strong, but they finish empty. They make you believe a harvest is coming, but what's left is barren ground.

But let me show you the other side. For every seed dropper, God still has fruit bearers. Fruit bearers are the ones who plant even when the soil looks hard. They water even when the ground looks dry. They stay consistent even when the season feels barren. Fruit bearers don't just show up for the praise break; they show up for the prayer meeting. They don't just shout for blessings, they sacrifice for holiness.

Jesus said in John 15:16, *"You have not chosen me, but I have chosen you, and ordained you, that ye should go and bring forth fruit, and that your fruit should remain."* Fruit bearers are chosen. They understand that their lives are not about temporary pleasure, but about an eternal purpose. They live with the awareness that what they plant today will bless generations to come.

The difference is simple. Seed droppers quit when it costs them something. Fruit bearers press on because they know the seed is worth the sacrifice. Seed droppers are satisfied with looking spiritual. Fruit bearers hunger to be transformed. Seed droppers leave the ground empty. Fruit bearers leave a legacy.

Tamar's story teaches us this truth. Onan dropped the seed, but God still honored Tamar with fruit. Out of her came Perez, an ancestor of David, and ultimately of Jesus Christ Himself. That means what one man dropped, God restored through His own plan. A seed dropper did not stop the lineage of the Messiah because fruit bearers will always rise.

So, ask yourself this: am I connected to seed droppers or fruit bearers? And even more important, which one am I? Because God is calling His people into a season where empty ground is no longer enough. He is raising fruit bearers, people who will commit, people who will stay, people who will plant when it is hard and rejoice when the harvest comes.

Friend, the call to wholeness is not about avoiding pain. It is about pressing through pain until your life produces something greater than what hurt you. The seed you carry is too valuable to waste. The ground God gave you is too rich to leave barren. This is your time to break free from seed droppers, take off your grave clothes, and step fully into the purpose God designed for you. Because in the Kingdom of God, it is not the seed droppers who change the world. It is the fruit bearers.

CHAPTER 4

Toxic Connections

Pain has a way of repeating itself. What hurt you yesterday can follow you into today if it goes unhealed. Left unchecked, pain becomes a cycle. You find yourself falling into the same kinds of relationships, the same disappointments, the same betrayals. You may change faces, addresses, or seasons, but the pattern looks familiar. It is the cycle of pain, and it is one of the enemy's greatest weapons to keep you bound.

There's also something strangely comfortable about toxic connections when you've been broken long enough. They confirm what you believe about yourself. They validate your worst fears. They prove your negative self-talk is right.

If you believe you're not worth investing in, freeloaders confirm it. If you believe you'll always be abandoned, seed droppers prove it. There's a twisted comfort in being right, even when being right means being broken.

This is why some people keep going back to the same type of toxic person over and over. It's not that they enjoy pain. It's that pain has become predictable, and predictable feels safer than unknown. Better the devil you know than the angel you don't, right? Wrong.

The Word tells us that spiritual impregnation comes only by being connected with others in Christ. But here's the warning: be careful who you connect with in the spiritual and natural. Not every connection is meant to conceive. Not every relationship is meant to birth purpose. Not every intimacy is meant to produce fruit.

When you connect with freeloaders and seed droppers, you go through all the motions of relationship without any of the fruit. You have the appearance of connection without the reality of it. You have the form of godliness but deny the power thereof.

In order to bear fruit, you must come together with the right people. You can pray by yourself. You can worship by yourself. You can sing by yourself. But in order for fruit to come, in order for purpose to be birthed, in order for destiny to be delivered, you must come together with people who won't freeload off your anointing or drop seed when it's time to commit.

Breaking Free from Toxic Connections

In Tamar's story, there was a third son, Shelah, whose name means "petition." Judah told Tamar to wait for him to grow up, to wait for the right time, to wait for the perfect circumstance. And Tamar waited. And waited. And waited.

Some of you are waiting for toxic people to change. You're waiting for the freeloader to start investing. You're waiting for the seed dropper to commit. You're waiting for someone to grow up and be who they promised they'd be.

But here's the truth: Judah never intended to give Shelah to Tamar. The promise was a lie to keep her quiet, to keep her waiting, to keep her from moving on. Sometimes toxic people make promises they never intend to keep just to keep you available for their dysfunction.

Tamar was not in the right mindset or position to receive Shelah anyway. She was still mourning. She was still in her grave clothes. She was still waiting for someone else to change her situation. Sometimes God withholds certain relationships not as punishment but as protection. You're not ready for healthy until you're done accepting toxic.

You must decide to break the chains and free yourself. Nobody else can do it for you. Your toxic connections won't release you voluntarily. Freeloaders don't suddenly start investing. Seed droppers don't magically become committed. You have to be the one to say, "Enough."

How bad do you want it? Because if you want wholeness, you have to be willing to be alone for a season. If you want healthy relationships, you have to be willing to let go of toxic ones. If you want people who invest, you have to stop subsidizing freeloaders. If you want people who commit, you have to stop accepting seed droppers.

The Power of Divine Disconnection

Sometimes the most spiritual thing you can do is disconnect. Sometimes the most holy action is to walk away. Sometimes the most faithful decision is to stop having faith in people who have proven they won't change.

Jesus himself said, "If anyone will not welcome you or listen to your words, leave that home or town and shake the dust off your feet." Even Jesus knew when to disconnect and walk away. Jesus knew that some connections aren't worth maintaining. You're not being mean when you disconnect from toxic people. You're being wise. You're being a good steward of your emotional and spiritual resources.

Once you disconnect from toxic connections, you need to set new standards for who you allow into your life. Not everyone deserves access to you, and neither has everyone earned the right to speak into your life.

At some point, you have to decide what you will and will not allow. Standards are not about arrogance; they are about self-respect. If someone refuses to invest in you, they should not have unlimited access to what you carry. If they will not commit to building with you, they should not get the benefits of being connected to you. If they refuse to plant seeds of love, loyalty, or consistency, they should not expect a harvest from your life. Relationships are not one-sided transactions. In the Kingdom, sowing and reaping are laws, not suggestions. Paul said it plainly in 2 Thessalonians 3:10, *"If anyone will not work, neither should he eat."*

The truth is, too many of us have been feeding people who never lift a finger, watering people who refuse to grow, and giving access to those who only take. And when you live like that, you drain yourself dry while they walk away full. That is not the will of God for you. Setting standards means recognizing your worth and protecting what God placed in you. It is saying, "I will no longer let seed-droppers enjoy the fruit of my tree."

Setting standards isn't about being rude or harsh, it's about protecting your emotional and spiritual well-being. These are biblical standards. These are healthy standards. These are the standards that will protect you from another generation of freeloaders and seed droppers.

Standards are not walls to keep people out, they are boundaries that protect what God has entrusted to you. Think of them as guardrails. Without them, you drift off course. With them, you stay aligned with His will.

The Word is clear about guarding your heart, for out of it flow the issues of life (Proverbs 4:23). The Bible warns us not to be unequally yoked (2 Corinthians 6:14). Jesus Himself told His disciples not to cast pearls before swine (Matthew 7:6). In other words, not everyone qualifies for access to the treasure inside of you.

Healthy standards keep you from repeating old cycles. They protect you from wasting years on people who only want what you have but never intend to pour back into you. They shield you from another generation of freeloaders who take without ever giving, and seed droppers who show up for the thrill but abandon you when it's time for fruit.

Think about it. When you set no standards, you give everybody a key to your house. Some will walk in respectfully, but others will come in and strip the place bare. Standards say, "Not here. Not anymore." They teach others how to treat you, and they remind you of the value God placed inside of you.

Never forget this truth: the people you allow into your life shape the direction of your life. If you surround yourself with freeloaders, you will always feel empty. If you stay tied to seed droppers, you will wonder why nothing ever grows. If you cling to toxic connections, you will never walk in the wholeness God designed for you.

Tamar's breakthrough came when she stopped waiting for toxic people to change. She realized she could not keep looking back, hoping Judah would finally do the right thing. At some point, she took off her widow's garments, her grave clothes, and positioned herself for blessing. She only received double for her trouble once she disconnected from the ones who had troubled her for nothing.

The same is true for you. Your wholeness is waiting on the other side of toxic disconnection. Your purpose is waiting on the other side of leaving dysfunction behind. Your destiny is waiting on the other side of raising your standards and refusing to settle for less than what God promised.

The choice is yours. The power is yours. The decision is yours. Choose wholeness. Choose freedom. Choose to disconnect from what drains you so you can connect with what builds you.

Your future is waiting. Your purpose is waiting. Your destiny is waiting. But first, you must clear the room. Disconnect from toxic people and situations. Stop allowing freeloaders and seed droppers to occupy the space meant for people who will invest, build, and grow with you.

It is time to change the company you keep. It is time to upgrade your connections. It is time to step into the wholeness you were created for.

CHAPTER 5

Don't Call Me Naomi

Let's sit with Naomi's story for a moment. I want you to feel it, not just read it. Because if we're honest, many of us have walked the same road she did.

The book of Ruth opens with promise and plenty. Naomi had a husband, Elimelech, two sons, and a home in Bethlehem, which literally means "the house of bread." Life was good. But then famine hit. And isn't that just like life? One day you're "successful," the next day you're "unprofitable." One day you're "healthy," the next day you're dealing with a terminal illness. One day you're "spouse," the next day you're "widow."

Life has a way of slapping labels on us based on our circumstances, and before we know it, we're introducing ourselves by our pain instead of our purpose. One moment you're secure, the next you're making choices you never thought you'd have to make.

Elimelech moved his family to Moab, a foreign land. It was supposed to be temporary. It was supposed to be survival.

But while in Moab, Naomi's world collapsed. First, her husband died. She still had her sons, though, and maybe she thought, *At least I have them. We'll rebuild.* But then, after ten years, both of her sons died too. Now she was a widow, childless, and living in a culture that saw women without men as worthless. The future she imagined was gone. The name Naomi, which means "pleasant," no longer seemed to fit her reality.

Life hit Naomi so hard that she told everybody to stop calling her by her given name. She said, "Don't call me Naomi. Call me Mara, because the Almighty has made my life very bitter." Have you ever been there? Have you ever felt like life handed you a name you didn't ask for? Maybe you started as "joyful," but life renamed you "weary." You started as "confident," but circumstances renamed you "insecure." You started as "loved," but betrayal renamed you "forgotten." We all at one point have allowed pain to change our identity.

I can certainly relate to Naomi's pain. I didn't lose a husband or a child, but life once hit so hard that I felt everything within me and around me was either dead or dying. But praise be to God, I am still here to tell the story of God's goodness! I can tell it, because I survived it. And I want to let you know that you will survive it, too. Whatever your It, may be, it will not kill you. It will not take you out. You will survive It!

I was once answering to names like, Broken. Bitter. Unworthy. Too Much. Not Enough. I, like so many others, was answering to the devil's labels and titles. But no matter what you answer to, God has not forgotten your name. The enemy wants you stuck in the label of your last storm, but God is calling you by the identity He gave you before the storm ever started.

Hear me today. You are not Mara. You are not Bitter. You are not Broken. You are Naomi. You are Pleasant. You are Purposeful. You are Whole. And you are still in God's plan.

Now watch what happens. Ruth 1:6 says, "Naomi arose with her daughters-in-law, preparing to leave Moab because she heard that the Lord had visited his people in her land and gave them bread." Naomi thought her story was over, but she didn't know God was writing a new chapter.

She felt that she had returned to Bethlehem empty, but what she didn't see was that she had Ruth, her daughter-in-law, with her.

Her judgment was off. Her perception was skewed. Her insight was limited by her pain. She had a messed-up perception of herself and her situation.

She said she came back empty, but she came back with Ruth. She said God had dealt bitterly with her, but God was setting her up for restoration. She said the Almighty had afflicted her, but the Almighty was about to bless her beyond her wildest dreams.

Don't let a distorted view of yourself or your situation rob you of the future God has promised. The enemy loves to whisper lies that everyone is against you, that the saints don't care, that your family has given up, or even that God Himself has turned His back. Those are lies designed to keep you stuck. Change the way you see yourself. Shift your perspective. Refuse to feed negativity. Like David, learn to encourage yourself in the Lord.

Ruth's loyalty led her to Boaz, and through their union came Obed, the grandfather of King David, and ultimately the lineage of Jesus Christ. Out of Naomi's bitterness came a blessing that would touch generations

Remember what God declares in Jeremiah 29:11: *"For I know the plans I have for you, says the Lord. They are plans for good and not disaster, to give you a future and a hope."* That means God has not forgotten you. He has not abandoned you. He has not stamped you with the label of your worst season. Yes, your winter may have felt long and cold, but spring is on its way. Your name may feel like Mara today, but Pleasant is still your portion.

Understanding Your Seasons

Listen, every living thing passes through seasons of change. Some seasons are easy, even pleasant to pass through. Others are difficult. So for those of you who feel as though you are stuck in a situation or a dilemma, you're not stuck. You're going through a cycle in your season that is about to change. Somebody, get ready for a wardrobe change!

Understanding your seasons, could be a whole chapter by itself, but I decided to include it with Naomi's chapter because she went through many seasons in her life.

I want you to understand that our God is a seasonal God. Solomon says in Ecclesiastes 3:1, *"To everything there is a season, and a time to every purpose under the heaven."*

Let's talk about some of the various seasons we experience in life.

1. The Planting Season – The Season of Beginnings
This is when you're sowing seeds of faith, discipline, and obedience, even though you don't see immediate results. It's the season of quiet beginnings, of learning to trust God with small steps.
Biblical Example: Abraham. When God told him to leave his homeland and go to a place He would show him (Genesis 12:1–4), Abraham planted seeds of obedience without yet knowing the harvest.

2. The Testing Season – The Season of Refinement
Life feels like a wilderness. You may be tested by trials, temptations, or seasons of silence where God seems far away. This is where your faith is refined like gold.
Biblical Example: Job. He endured unimaginable suffering and loss, yet held on to his faith, declaring, "Though He slay me, yet will I trust Him" (Job 13:15).

3. The Blooming Season – The Season of Visible Growth

This is when the seeds you planted begin to sprout. Opportunities open, relationships flourish, and your faith comes alive. It's when others start to see the fruit of your obedience.

Biblical Example: Joseph. After years of waiting and testing, Joseph moved from the prison to the palace. What was hidden in obscurity was revealed in God's timing (Genesis 41).

4. The Pruning Season – The Season of Cutting Back

This is when God removes things from your life, not to punish you, but to prepare you for greater fruitfulness. It might be people, habits, or old ways of thinking. It feels like a loss, but it's actually growth.

Biblical Example: Ruth. She lost her husband and left her homeland, but in that pruning came new purpose and a connection to Boaz, which placed her in the lineage of Christ (Ruth 1–4).

5. The Waiting Season – The Season of Preparation
It feels quiet, even stagnant, but beneath the surface God is building roots. Waiting is never wasted when it's in God's hands. He is strengthening you for what's ahead.
Biblical Example: David. Anointed as king while still a shepherd boy, David had to wait years before sitting on the throne. In the meantime, God used the waiting season to prepare him (1 Samuel 16).

6. The Harvest Season – The Season of Reaping
This is the season of reward. You see the results of faith, endurance, and obedience. The harvest can be joy, breakthrough, ministry fruit, or restoration.
Biblical Example: Hannah. After years of barrenness and prayer, she gave birth to Samuel, the prophet who would anoint kings. Her harvest came after a long season of waiting and weeping.(1 Samuel 1–2).

Listen, seasons aren't just something that happens to you; they aren't random. They are something God uses to shape you. Each one comes with an assignment. The planting season is where God builds your faith muscle. You can't see anything yet, but you have to believe something's happening underground. The waiting season, that's where your patience gets stretched like taffy until you think you're going to snap, but you don't. You grow instead. The pruning season? That's where God cuts away everything that's sucking life from you, and it hurts like hell, but it strengthens your character in ways comfort never could. The blooming season proves that every tear, every prayer, every sleepless night was worth it. And the harvest season? That's God's way of saying, "I told you I was faithful. Did you doubt Me?"

Look at Naomi's life. She started in Bethlehem, which literally means "house of bread." She had bread in the house of bread. She was living in overflow, in a season of plenty where everything made sense and life was good. But then famine hit. Not a little shortage, but the kind of famine that makes you pack up everything and leave for a foreign land. That move to Moab? That was her winter season. A season of just trying to survive, of making it through another day, of feeling like God was a million miles away when He used to feel close enough to touch.

In Moab, winter turned into something worse. Her husband Elimelech died. Then both her sons, Mahlon and Chilion, died. Can you imagine? That wasn't just winter anymore; that was her pruning season. And let me tell you something about pruning: it feels like death. It feels like everything you loved and everything you built your life on is being cut away with no mercy. That's why she renamed herself, Mara. Mara means, "bitter," because she felt hollowed out, emptied, forgotten by the very God who was supposed to protect her.

But here's what Naomi couldn't see in her bitterness: God was working. Even in Moab. Even in the deaths. Even in the emptiness. When she heard that the Lord had visited His people back in Bethlehem and given them bread, something rose up in her. Ruth 1:6 says she "arose." That's not just getting up physically. That's your spirit recognizing a shift before your mind catches up. She moved from the season of loss into a season of refreshing, even though all she could feel was pain.

Naomi thought her story was a tragedy ending in winter's grip, but God was already writing spring into her story. She thought famine was her finale, but fruitfulness was waiting in Bethlehem with her name on it. The season that felt empty was actually pregnant with a generational blessing that would change the world.

So why do we go through seasons? Because God isn't trying to make you comfortable; He's trying to make you complete. He uses seasons to strip away what can't go where He's taking you. That relationship that died in your winter? It couldn't survive in your spring. That job you lost in your pruning? It was too small for your harvest. He uses seasons to reveal whether your faith is in your circumstances or in Him. And He uses them to show you that your life isn't about one moment, one season, one chapter. It's about the entire story He's writing, and honey, He's not done writing yet.

How do you navigate your seasons? You remember what Naomi had to learn the hard way: God hasn't forgotten you. He can't forget you. You're engraved on the palms of His hands. When famine comes, you don't let go of His hand. When loss hits, you grieve, you cry, you scream if you need to, but you don't quit. When bitterness tries to rename you, you remind yourself that Pleasant is still your portion, still your inheritance, still your true name. When God calls you back to your Bethlehem, to your place of purpose, you get up and you go. Even if you're limping. Even if you're crying. Even if all you've got is a Ruth holding onto your hem.

You trust that winter is not forever. Spring is not just coming; it's inevitable. Every season you've survived is preparing you for a harvest you can't even imagine yet.

Here's what I need you to hear: whatever season you're in right now, it's not your conclusion. It's your preparation. Naomi's winter was bitter enough to change her name, but her spring carried the DNA of the Messiah. Your winter might be brutal, but your spring will birth something that will outlive you. God is still writing your story, and your next season isn't just on the horizon. It's already in motion.

The seeds are already underground. The shift has already started. Your refreshing is closer than you think. Hold on. Spring is coming. And it's bringing more than you lost.

There are elements that can make you miss your season of refreshing:

Your Past. Everyone has a past. The devil uses it to intimidate believers. There are so many highly gifted, anointed women and men who are not operating in their gifts because of fear and intimidation. The devil will make you feel paranoid when you see someone looking at you and smiling, thinking "they knew you when." Yes, your past is just that: past. Don't let it keep you from your season.

Your Quandary. Your dilemma, tight spot, jam, pickle, catch-22. Your difficult or tricky situation shouldn't make you immovable in your present. Naomi was old and alone. Now that's a dilemma. But she arose anyway.

Your Judgment. Your perception, your insight, or lack of discernment. This is what almost kept Naomi back. She saw herself as empty when she was actually carrying seed for the future.

A productive season is the period of time when you are most fruitful and abundant. You don't have to work as hard; things just flow. But here's what many don't understand: there's a purging process before the productive season.

Just like a woman's body has cycles, after ovulation, if nothing is seeded, then your next cycle will begin, which pushes out the dead stuff and the impurities and will get you ready for another season to be fruitful.

God has created us so that if no seed impregnates us, it doesn't stay in us. All the dead stuff is purged out. God has a way of purging us in the pain, pressure, and discomfort through His cleansing process to get us ready for fruit.

Your Moab season, your bitter season, your Mara season, it's not punishment. It's purging. It's preparation. It's God getting you ready for something so good that you needed to be emptied first to have room to receive it.

By the end of the book of Ruth, Naomi is holding her grandson, Obed, who would become the grandfather of King David, the lineage of Jesus Christ. The women of the town said to her, *"Blessed be the Lord, who has not left you without a redeemer today. May his name become famous in Israel. He will renew your life and sustain you in your old age."*

The woman who said "call me Bitter" became the woman they called Blessed. The woman who said she came back empty became full again. The woman who thought God was against her discovered God had been working for her all along.

Your season represents what God has placed within you. Don't miscarry it. Don't abort it. For some of you, your delivery date is past due, and for others, don't miss your due date. Guard what God has planted in you; speak life over it. Walk into your season.

As we close this chapter, I want you to do something. I want you to say your real name out loud. Not the name life gave you. Not the name pain gave you. Not the name loss gave you. Say the name God gave you.

"I am not Mara. I am Naomi." "I am not bitter. I am blessed." "I am not empty. I am full." "I am not forgotten. I am favored." "I am not finished. I am just getting started."

Don't let anybody, including yourself, call you by a name God didn't give you. Don't let your worst season become your permanent identity. Don't let your Moab become your mailing address.

You may have lost much. You may have been through hell and high water. You may have scars that tell stories you don't want to repeat. But you're still here. You survived. And if God kept you alive, He kept you alive for a reason.

Your new season is here. Your refreshing has come. Your name is being restored. Not the name pain gave you, but the name purpose is calling you.

Rise up like Naomi did when she heard the Lord had visited His people with bread. Rise up and return to your place of purpose. Rise up and walk into your season of refreshing.

And when people see you coming, when they notice the change, when they ask, "Can this be you?" Don't tell them about Mara. Tell them about mercy. Don't testify about bitter. Testify about better. Don't rehearse the pain. Proclaim the promise.

Your winter has been long, but spring has sprung. Your season is shifting. Your name is changing back. Not to what it was, but to something even better.

Know your season. Prepare for your season. Walk into your season. And don't let anybody call you out of your name, unless they are calling you blessed!

CHAPTER 6

Pressed But Not Crushed

Here's what I've learned about God's mathematics: He never allows more pressure than what will produce purpose. He never permits more pressure than what will produce power. He never sanctions more squeezing than what will produce strength.

When grapes are pressed, they produce wine. When olives are pressed, they release oil. When flowers are pressed, they release fragrance. And when you are pressed, you produce something too. The question is, what is coming out of you under pressure?

For some, pressure reveals bitterness, anger, or doubt. For others, pressure reveals faith, resilience, and worship. Pressure exposes what was already inside. It shows what you've been cultivating in the quiet seasons. When you are pressed and what comes out is prayer, that means prayer was already in you. When you are pressed and what comes out is worship, that means worship was already planted in your spirit. When you are pressed and faith rises up instead of fear, that means faith has been growing under the surface.

This is why pressure is not your enemy. It is the proving ground of your destiny. Without pressure, you would never know how strong your praise really is. Without pressure, you would never discover the depth of your faith. Without pressure, you would not realize that what God deposited in you is unshakable.

Think about Paul and Silas in Acts 16. They were beaten and thrown into a Philippian jail, their bodies aching, their feet locked in stocks. That is pressure. But what came out of them was not despair, not complaining, not bitterness. At midnight, the Bible says, they prayed and sang hymns to God, and the prisoners were listening. And suddenly there was an earthquake that shook the foundations of the prison, opened every door, and loosed every chain. That was the power of praise under pressure.

What was produced in that prison was not just their deliverance, but the salvation of the jailer and his entire household. When they were pressed, their worship became a weapon, and that weapon broke chains not only for themselves but for everyone around them.

So when you are pressed, understand this: something bigger than you is being produced. Your praise under pressure encourages someone else who is watching you. Your faith under pressure becomes the testimony that breaks somebody else's chains. Your survival under pressure declares to the world that God is still faithful.

The pressing is not punishment. It is preparation. It is not destruction. It is development. It is not the end of your story. It is the part where your story gains its power.

If pressure reveals what's inside, then the wise thing to do is start cultivating the right things before the press comes. Here are four practices that will prepare you for the seasons when life squeezes:

1. Cultivate Prayer Daily

Prayer is more than asking God for things. It's building relationship with Him. When prayer becomes your habit, it will also become your reflex. That means when pressure shows up, instead of panicking, your spirit will automatically turn to God. Daniel prayed three times a day even when the king's decree threatened his life. So when pressure came, his response was already prepared.

2. Fill Yourself with the Word

What you store in your heart is what will come out of your mouth when life presses you. If all you consume is negativity, doubt will come out under pressure. But if you fill your mind and spirit with God's Word, His promises will rise up when you need them most. Jesus modeled this in the wilderness when the enemy tried to tempt Him. He answered every attack with "It is written." Pressure revealed what He had hidden in His heart.

3. Practice Praise in Every Season

Praise in the easy seasons makes praise natural in the hard ones. Don't wait until your back is against the wall to learn how to worship. Praise God in the small things now, so when the storm hits, you already know how to lift your hands. Paul and Silas didn't start praising in the jail out of nowhere. They had a lifestyle of worship that flowed out of them under pressure.

4. Build Healthy Connections

The people around you will influence how you respond when life presses you. If doubters surround you, their fear will feed your fear. But if you are surrounded by faith-filled believers, their strength will feed your strength. Naomi had Ruth, and Ruth's loyalty kept Naomi from giving up in bitterness. Choose companions who will remind you of God's promises when you forget.

So do not despise the press. Use your today to prepare for your tomorrow. Fill yourself with prayer, the Word, praise, and healthy connections so that when life presses you, what comes out is faith, worship, and strength. That way, the press will not destroy you. It will only reveal what God has already placed inside you.

You're Still Here

You're still here, and it's not by accident either. You're still here because you survived. God kept you. You made it through the crushing! Now, let me tell you something about survivors that nobody talks about. We don't always look victorious. Sometimes we look like we've been through hell and back, because we have. You know the cliché, *'I don't look like what I've been through.'* Well, that's not true for everyone. Sometimes, we look exactly like what we've been through, or in some instances, what we are currently going through. But the thing about survivors is this: we're still standing. And in the kingdom of God, still standing is a form of praise.

You might be reading this with tears in your eyes, gripping the pages and wondering if simply surviving is enough. Let me tell you right now: Yes, it is. Your survival is not second place. It is not a consolation prize. It is proof. Proof that what came to destroy you didn't win. Proof that God's hand has been on your life even in the moments you couldn't feel Him.

Think about it. You have survived things that should have buried you. A divorce that tried to crush you. An illness that threatened to end your life. Depression that tried to swallow you whole. Abuse that could have broken you beyond repair. Betrayal that made you question whether you could ever love again. Yet, here you are. Still standing. Still breathing. Still reading these words. That's not an accident. That's a testimony.

Let's talk about Joseph. This young man's survival story spans seventeen years. It starts in Genesis 37 when he's seventeen years old, wearing a coat of many colors, having dreams of greatness. His brothers hate him so much they throw him in a pit and sell him into slavery.

Think about that pit for a moment. Joseph is at the bottom, probably crying out, hearing his brothers eating lunch above him while deciding whether to kill him or sell him. That pit should have been his grave. But he survived.

He becomes a slave in Potiphar's house. Just when things start looking up, Potiphar's wife lies about him, accuses him of attempted rape, and he ends up in prison. Genesis 39:20 says he was put in the king's prison, the place where the king's prisoners were confined. This wasn't minimum security. This was the dungeon.

In prison, Joseph interprets dreams for the butler and baker. The butler promises to remember Joseph when he gets out. But Genesis 40:23 tells us, *"Yet the chief butler did not remember Joseph, but forgot him."* Two more years pass. Forgotten. Abandoned. Still in prison.

But Joseph survived. And when Pharaoh needed a dream interpreted, suddenly Joseph goes from the prison to the palace in one day. From prisoner to Prime Minister. From forgotten to favored. By Genesis 41:40, Pharaoh is saying, *"You shall be over my house, and all my people shall be ruled according to your word."*

Thirteen years. That's how long Joseph's survival season lasted. Thirteen years of betrayal, slavery, false accusation, and imprisonment. But his survival positioned him to save nations from famine, including the very brothers who tried to destroy him.

Hannah survived a season of barrenness. I Samuel introduces us to Hannah, a woman surviving a different kind of pain. She's barren in a culture where a woman's worth was measured by her ability to produce children. Her husband's other wife, Peninnah, has children and torments Hannah about her barrenness year after year.

1 Samuel 1:6-7 says Peninnah *"provoked her severely, to make her miserable... so it was, year by year."* This wasn't a one-time hurt. This was ongoing emotional torture. Hannah was surviving daily humiliation, monthly disappointment, and yearly torment. Can you imagine the emotional agony she had to endure?

But Hannah did something powerful. She took her survival to the temple. 1Samuel 1:10 says she was "in bitterness of soul, and prayed to the Lord and wept in anguish." She wasn't pretty in her prayers. She was honest. She was raw. She was surviving by pouring out her pain before God.

And God remembered Hannah. She gave birth to Samuel, who became one of Israel's greatest prophets. But here's what I love: After Samuel was born, Hannah didn't just celebrate her personal victory. She prayed a prayer in 1 Samuel 2 that became a prophecy about God lifting up all the lowly, feeding all the hungry, and strengthening all the weak.

Her survival became a song for other survivors. Her breakthrough became a blessing for others who were broken.

Now I can't talk about survival without mentioning Apostle Paul. If anybody knew about surviving, it was Paul. In 2 Corinthians 11:24-28, he gives us his survival resume:

"Five times I received forty stripes minus one. Three times I was beaten with rods; once I was stoned; three times I was shipwrecked; a night and a day I have been in the deep; in journeys often, in perils of waters, in perils of robbers, in perils of my own countrymen, in perils of the Gentiles, in perils in the city, in perils in the wilderness, in perils in the sea, in perils among false brethren; in weariness and toil, in sleeplessness often, in hunger and thirst, in fasting often, in cold and nakedness."

That's not a testimony; that's a trauma list. Any one of those things could have killed him. But Paul survived them all. And here's what he says about it in 2 Corinthians 4:8-9:

"We are hard-pressed on every side, yet not crushed; we are perplexed, but not in despair; persecuted, but not forsaken; struck down, but not destroyed."

That's the anthem of survivors. Pressed but not crushed. Confused but not giving up. Hunted but not abandoned. Knocked down but not knocked out.

When you look at the lives of these biblical survivors, a pattern starts to stand out. Every one of them faced circumstances that could have ended their story. Each one had seasons of fear, doubt, and deep questions. They all experienced betrayal, opposition, or abandonment. Yet they shared one common thread: they refused to let their circumstances have the final word.

Job could have given up and cursed God, just like his wife told him to. Joseph could have let bitterness eat him alive in that prison cell. Hannah could have let barrenness define her future. Paul could have thrown in the towel after the first beating.

But they didn't. They kept standing. They endured. They pressed on. Not because they were extraordinary people with superhuman strength, but because they were carried by a supernatural God. Their survival was not about their ability. It was about God's faithfulness.

And here's the part I don't want you to miss: the same God who carried them is the same God who is carrying you. How do I know, because he's the same yesterday, today, and forever. God doesn't play favorites. Just as He sustained Job in his season of loss, He will sustain you in your season of grief. The same way He raised Joseph from the prison to the palace, He can lift you out of the pit you feel stuck in right now.

In the same way God remembered Hannah and gave her the desire of her heart, He will not forget you. Just as He gave Paul the strength to rise again after shipwrecks, beatings, and disappointments, He will give you the strength to rise after every setback. You may feel pressed on every side, but you are not crushed. You may feel struck down, but you are not destroyed. You may have felt like giving up, but here you are, still standing because God has been holding you up all along.

And now, let's bring this closer to home. Your pit may not look like Joseph's, but you know what it feels like to be at the bottom while others stood over you as if your future was theirs to decide. Your furnace may not be fiery like the Hebrew boys,' but you know the heat of trials so intense you wondered if they would burn you alive. Your barrenness may not be about children like Hannah's, but you know what it is to watch dreams miscarry, promises delay, and hope feel like it slipped through your fingers. Your thorn may not be Paul's, but you know what it is to carry pain that refuses to leave, no matter how much you pray.

You are not alone in this. You are in good company. Scripture is filled with survivors who looked like failures before they looked like champions. Survivors who sat in pits before they stood in palaces. Survivors who walked through flames before they walked in promise. Survivors who endured seasons of emptiness before giving birth to destiny.

And here is what they teach us: survival seasons are never wasted. God uses them to prepare us for significance. Joseph's pit prepared him for Pharaoh's palace. The Hebrew boys' furnace prepared them for promotion in Babylon. Hannah's barrenness prepared her to raise a prophet. Paul's sufferings prepared him to write words that still encourage us today. Job's losses prepared him to model endurance for generations.

So do not despise your survival story. Every test has been shaping a testimony. Every trial has been working truth into your soul. Every struggle has been building strength for the next level of your purpose. The fact that you are here, reading these words, is proof that survival is not small. It is not weak. It is victory!

Look at yourself. Look at your scars. Look at your story. You are still here. And if God brought you this far, He is not done with you yet. Rejoice in your survival, because survival is the seed of significance. You made it through the fire, through the storm, through the pit, through the pain. And if you survived that, you are more than ready for what God has next.

CHAPTER 7

God's Restoration Plan

There's something about broken things that makes us want to throw them away. A broken plate goes in the trash. A broken phone gets replaced. A broken relationship gets abandoned. We live in a disposable culture that says broken means done, shattered means finished, damaged means discarded.

Brokenness is also something every one of us understands because life has a way of leaving cracks in our hearts and scars on our souls. Maybe it was a relationship that left you shattered. Perhaps it was a betrayal that broke your trust. The years of struggling with loss, disappointment, or rejection. Whatever it was, it left you feeling broken and like pieces of you were missing.

Here's the good news: God has a restoration plan. Throughout Scripture, He shows himself as the God who specializes in restoration. Not just fixing what's broken, but making it better than it was before. He doesn't just repair the damage, but uses the damage to create something more beautiful than the original.

He is not intimidated by broken pieces. In fact, He specializes in taking what looks ruined and putting it back together better than before. Psalm 34:18 tells us, *"The Lord is close to the brokenhearted and saves those who are crushed in spirit."* Notice what that means: God draws near to brokenness. Where others may walk away from the mess, God steps in.

The Japanese have an art form called Kintsugi, where broken pottery is repaired with gold. The breaking isn't hidden; it's highlighted. The repair doesn't disguise the damage; it celebrates the restoration. The item becomes more valuable after it's been broken and restored than it ever was in its original state.

That's what God does with our broken lives. He doesn't just glue us back together and hope nobody notices the cracks. He fills our cracks with glory. He turns our broken places into our most beautiful features. He makes our restoration story more powerful than our original story ever could have been. The places that once embarrassed you become the very places that testify to His power!

Let's return to Tamar one more time, because her story is the ultimate picture of God restoring what was broken. This woman's life was shattered piece by piece. Her first marriage, broken by death. Her second marriage, broken by betrayal. Her promise of a third marriage, broken by deception. Her reputation, broken by circumstances. Her future, broken by cultural limitations.

She was a collection of broken pieces. Broken dreams of motherhood. Broken hopes of security. Broken expectations of family. Everything that mattered in her culture, everything that gave a woman value in her time, was broken in her life.

But God specializes in restoration that exceeds imagination. When Tamar revealed to Judah that she was pregnant with his children, when he declared "She has been more righteous than I," something shifted in the spiritual realm. The broken woman was about to become the restored woman. The shattered vessel was about to become the carrier of kings.

Genesis 38:27 tells us, *"When the time came for her to give birth, there were twin boys in her womb."* Not one baby to replace what she lost, but two. Not just restoration, but multiplication. Not just fixing what was broken, but creating something that had never existed before.

In the New Testament, John chapter 4 introduces us to a woman whose entire life was a series of broken relationships and public rejections. She comes to Jacob's well at noon, the hottest part of the day, when nobody else would be there. Let that sink in. She structured her entire day around avoiding people. She chose physical discomfort over social interaction. She picked scorching heat over human contact.

Why? Because shame had become her companion, and isolation had become her protection. I'm sure the town knew her story. They knew all about her broken relationships. Therefore, she could have been the talk of the town. You know how people love to talk about someone else's issues and sins, all while drowning in their own sea of iniquity.

The Bible tells us she had five husbands, and the man she was currently with wasn't her husband. Now before we judge her, understand that in her culture, women couldn't initiate divorce. Those five husbands? They rejected her. They discarded her. They passed her around like she was property that kept depreciating in value. By the time we meet her, she's just living with someone, probably because no one would offer her the dignity of marriage.

This woman knew what it was like to be broken by rejection. To have hope five times and lose it five times. To believe "this time will be different" only to end up dismissed again. She was the town scandal, the cautionary tale mothers told their daughters, the woman respectable people crossed the street to avoid.

But Jesus was waiting for her at that well. Not accidentally. Not coincidentally. Intentionally. John 4:4 says, "He had to go through Samaria." Jews didn't have to go through Samaria. They usually went around it to avoid the Samaritans altogether. But Jesus had an appointment with a broken woman who thought she was just coming to get water.

Jesus starts with a simple request: "Give me a drink." A Jewish rabbi was speaking to a Samaritan woman. A holy man was acknowledging someone considered unholy. A man was treating her like a human being, not a scandal.

She's shocked. "How is it that you, being a Jew, ask a drink from me, a Samaritan woman?" She's basically saying, "Don't you know who I am? Don't you know I'm untouchable? Don't you know my reputation?"

But Jesus doesn't care about her reputation. He cares about her restoration. He tells her about living water, water that would become a fountain springing up into everlasting life. She wants this water, thinking it means she'll never have to come to this well again, never have to face the daily shame of isolation.

Then Jesus does something remarkable. He says, "Go, call your husband."

This is the moment where most of us would run. This is where shame would usually win. She could have lied. She could have made excuses and walked away. Instead, she tells the truth: "I have no husband."

And Jesus responds with something that should have destroyed her, but instead delivered her: "You have well said, 'I have no husband,' for you have had five husbands, and the one whom you now have is not your husband."

This is the pivotal moment. Jesus knew everything about her before He asked for water. He knew about all five rejections. He knew about the current situation. He knew about the shame. Yet, he engaged with her anyway.

For the first time in her life, someone saw all of her and didn't walk away. Someone knew her whole story and didn't reject her. Someone understood her complete brokenness and offered her living water instead of judgment. Jesus didn't accidentally bump into her. He intentionally positioned Himself in her path. He orchestrated a divine appointment with a woman who had given up on divine anything.

When you've been rejected five times, you stop expecting acceptance. When you've been discarded repeatedly, you stop believing you have value. When shame becomes your identity, you stop imagining you could be anything else. But Jesus specializes in restoring what rejection has ruined.

Watch what happens next. The woman starts talking theology, bringing up worship and mountains and ancestors. But Jesus cuts through all that religious talk and gets to the heart of the matter. He reveals Himself as the Messiah.

Think about that. Jesus revealed His identity as the Messiah to a rejected Samaritan woman before He revealed it to most of His disciples. Why? Because restoration isn't just about fixing what's broken; it's also about elevating what's been diminished.

Wounded by rejection and broken by failed relationships, she came to the well hiding in shame. But one conversation with Jesus restored her identity. She left her water jar behind and ran to tell her whole town about the Messiah. John 4:28 tells us something profound: "The woman then left her waterpot, went her way into the city."

She left her water jar. The very thing she came for, she abandoned. The vessel that represented her daily shame, her noon isolation, her careful avoidance of people, she left it behind. Why? Because when you've tasted living water, you don't need to carry empty vessels anymore. When you've found what truly satisfies, you don't need to keep going back to what never did.

That water jar represented her old life. Her routine of shame. Her pattern of hiding. Her acceptance of rejection as normal. But one conversation with Jesus made all of that obsolete. She didn't need to hide anymore because she had been seen and accepted. She didn't need to avoid people anymore because she had been validated by the Messiah Himself.

Rejected by people and scarred by one failed relationship after another, she showed up at the well in the heat of the day, hoping no one would notice her. She came carrying shame heavier than the water jar on her shoulder. But one encounter with Jesus changed everything. With just a few words, He reached past her past and spoke to the core of who she was. Her identity was restored, her dignity renewed. She came looking for water, but she left overflowing. She dropped her jar and ran back to the very people she once avoided, boldly declaring, "Come see a man who told me everything I ever did." The woman who hid in shame became the first evangelist in her city.

Just like the woman at the well, some of you have been trying to satisfy your soul-thirst at broken wells. You've been looking for living water in relationships that only offer temporary refreshment. You've been seeking satisfaction in all the wrong places, but you keep having to come back to the well because nothing satisfies you for long.

Jesus offers water that becomes a fountain within you. Not water you have to keep going back for, but water that springs up from inside. Not satisfaction that depends on external circumstances, but satisfaction that flows from internal transformation.

When Jesus restores you at your well, your testimony becomes powerful. The woman's testimony was simple: "Come see a man who told me everything I ever did." She didn't have a theology degree or a perfect reputation. She had an encounter, and that was enough.

Running to Tell Your City

When God restores you, it is impossible to stay silent. Restoration has a way of spilling over. Look at the woman at the well. The same woman who once avoided her city ran back to it, shouting the good news. The one who had been whispered about as the town's shame became the very vessel God used to bless the whole community. The one everyone had written off as an example of failure became the proof of what grace can do.

And it is the same with you. Your restoration is not just about you. It is a message for the people around you. Your family needs to see that shame does not get the last word. Your friends need to see that broken pieces can be made whole. Your workplace needs to see that faith can transform a life. Even your social media needs to testify that hiding seasons can become healing seasons.

So do not hide your story just because it has messy chapters. The woman at the well, used her brokenness as her sermon. "He told me everything I ever did," she said. And included in that "everything" was five failed marriages and the man she was living with, who was not her husband. But included in that "everything" was also divine acceptance, living water, and a brand-new identity.

Your restoration story is not something to be ashamed of. It is evidence that God still heals, still redeems, and still transforms.

Jesus visits wells, waiting for broken women and men who are just trying to survive another day. He's still offering living water to those whose wells have run dry. He's still restoring those whom the world has rejected repeatedly.

Come to the well. Meet Him there. Tell Him the truth about your situation. Receive the living water. Leave your jar. Run to your city.

Your restoration story is someone else's hope. Your testimony is someone else's breakthrough. Your healing is someone else's permission to believe healing is possible.

The woman at the well became the woman with the well of living water within her. That can be your story too.

A Prayer for the Woman at the Well in You

"Lord Jesus, I come to my well right now, in the heat of my shame, in the isolation of my rejection, in the brokenness of my repeated failures. I've been hiding, avoiding, protecting myself from more hurt.

But You're here waiting for me. You know everything I've done, every relationship that's failed, every rejection I've experienced, every shameful secret I carry, and You're still here. Still offering living water. Still offering restoration.

I receive Your living water. I let it become a fountain in me. I let it satisfy the thirst that no human relationship could quench. I let it wash away the shame that has kept me in hiding.

I leave my water jar at this well. I leave my old patterns, my shame routines, my isolation habits. I pick up my testimony. I pick up my restoration. I pick up my new identity.

Give me courage to run to my city. Give me boldness to tell my story. Give me faith to believe that my restoration can trigger revival for others.

Thank You for meeting me at my well. Thank You for seeing all of me and loving me anyway. Thank You for restoration that exceeds my rejection.

In Jesus's name, Amen."

CHAPTER 8

Treasures, Not Trash: Reclaiming Your True Value

Somewhere along the way, life tried to convince you that you are less than who God says you are. Therefore, we need to address something fundamental: you've been treating treasure like trash, and it's time to reclaim your true value.

Second Corinthians 4:7 says, *"But we have this treasure in earthen vessels, that the excellency of the power may be of God and not of us."* Did you catch that? You're not trash carrying trash. You're an earthen vessel carrying treasure. You might be made of dirt, but what's inside you is divine. You might be fragile, but what you're carrying is forceful. You might be common clay, but your contents are Kingdom gold.

The problem is many of us have been living like we're the trash instead of recognizing we're the treasury. We've been apologizing for existing instead of acknowledging our value. We've been accepting treatment that belongs in a dumpster instead of demanding the respect that belongs to a treasure.

Understanding Your Spiritual DNA

Inside each of us is something greater than blood, greater than genetics, greater than heritage—it's called spiritual DNA. This is what connects you directly to your Creator. When God breathed His breath into Adam (Genesis 2:7), He transferred divine essence into humanity. That breath is still flowing in you today.

Your spiritual DNA carries the attributes of your Father. Just like children have the features of their parents, you also have the nature of God within you. That means creativity is in you because He is the Creator. Strength is in you because He is strong. Love is in you because He is love. Wisdom, compassion, endurance, all of it is already encoded in your spiritual DNA.

When you accepted Christ, that DNA was reactivated. 2 Corinthians 5:17 says, *"If anyone is in Christ, he is a new creation. The old has passed away; behold, the new has come."* Salvation didn't just change your destination; it changed your nature. You are no longer bound by the limits of who you used to be. The same Spirit that raised Jesus from the dead lives in you (Romans 8:11). That means resurrection power runs through your spiritual bloodstream.

But here's the problem too many of us live like spiritual orphans, unaware of the royal DNA that we carry. We chase validation from people when we already have affirmation from heaven. We look for worth in relationships, status, or success, forgetting that our value was determined before we ever entered the room.

Jesus told a story in Matthew 13:44: *"The kingdom of heaven is like treasure hidden in a field. When a man found it, he hid it again, and then in his joy went and sold all he had and bought that field."* The treasure represents you. The field represents the world. And the man who bought the field is God Himself. He saw your worth buried beneath dirt, pain, and sin, and He paid the ultimate price—His Son—to redeem you. God didn't just see your value; He pursued it.

You may have been buried under mistakes or hidden by circumstances, but treasure doesn't stop being treasure just because it's covered in dirt. God digs until He finds you. He cleanses you. He restores you. And then He puts you on display as evidence of His grace.

Recognizing the Value Within

Once you understand your spiritual DNA, you start seeing yourself differently. You stop entertaining relationships that devalue you. You stop comparing your process to someone else's highlight reel. You start walking with confidence, knowing that God placed treasure inside of you.

You are not trying to become valuable; you are uncovering the value that was there all along. Like Tamar, who was cast aside but chosen to be part of Jesus' lineage, your story is proof that God specializes in pulling treasure out of what others called trash. Her rejection didn't define her; God's restoration did.

Maybe you've spent years in places that didn't recognize your worth. Maybe people treated you like you were replaceable. But God has never stopped seeing you as His treasure. Isaiah 62:3 declares, *"You shall also be a crown of glory in the hand of the Lord, and a royal diadem in the hand of your God."* You are not ordinary. You are royalty in divine hands.

Knowing your value is one thing; walking in it is another. When you truly believe you are a treasure, you stop settling. You protect your peace. You guard your time. You stop auditioning for acceptance and start walking in purpose.

Living like a treasure means embracing your spiritual DNA every day. It means waking up and saying, "I am fearfully and wonderfully made." It means trusting that even when life tries to devalue you, heaven's record still declares you priceless. It means refusing to live beneath what God already paid for.

You don't have to strive to be valuable. You were valuable when God formed you. You were valuable when He called you by name. You were valuable when Jesus hung on the cross and said, "It is finished." That was heaven's receipt, proof that your value is non-negotiable.

So how do you start living like treasure instead of trash? It begins with activation. Your spiritual DNA is already there—it just needs to be awakened. The treasure is in you, but you have to start treating yourself like you believe it.

Step One: Change Your Language.

Words create worlds. What you speak shapes what you see. Stop canceling your value with negative talk. God didn't call you "just" anything. He called you chosen, royal, and set apart. So stop saying:

"I'm just trying to get by."

"I'm only one person."

"I'm nothing special."

"I don't matter."

"I'm not important."

And start declaring truth:

"I'm carrying treasure."

"I have value."

"I'm made in God's image."

"My life has purpose."

"I matter deeply to God."

When your words align with God's Word, your mindset begins to shift. You stop living like trash because your spirit remembers it was born of treasure.

Step Two: Change Your Standards.

Treasure doesn't belong in the trash. You can't claim value while tolerating what diminishes you. Start setting boundaries that match your worth. Stop accepting:

Disrespect disguised as humor.

Neglect disguised as busyness.

Abuse disguised as love.

Manipulation disguised as concern.

Devaluation disguised as humility.

You teach others how to treat you by how you treat yourself. When you remember your value, you stop settling for scraps when God already set a table.

Once you recognize you're treasure, you have to maintain that recognition. The world will constantly try to convince you otherwise. People who are comfortable with you being trash will be uncomfortable with you being treasure.

Here's how to maintain your treasure identity:

Feed your spiritual DNA daily. Read the Word. Pray. Worship. These aren't just religious activities; they're DNA maintenance. They keep your spiritual genetics strong.

Surround yourself with others who recognize treasure. You need a community that sees your value, not one that constantly questions it. Iron sharpens iron, and treasure recognizes treasure.

Practice saying no. Treasure is selective about where it goes and who has access to it. You can't be available for every request, every event, every person who wants a piece of you.

As we close this chapter, remember this: your treasure story isn't just about you. People are watching your life who have only ever known "trash treatment." They've been tossed aside, talked down to, and made to feel small. They need to see someone like you who dares to believe they are a treasure. Someone who refuses to accept disrespect or devaluation. Someone who stands tall in their worth and reminds the world that value isn't earned; it's inherited from God.

Paul wrote in Philippians 3:8, *"I consider everything a loss because of the surpassing worth of knowing Christ Jesus my Lord."* He understood that when you know who you belong to, you stop questioning your worth.

You are not trash that somehow got lucky. You are not garbage that God decided to upgrade. You are a treasure that has finally been revealed. You've always been a treasure; it just took a little time for you to remember.

And now, you do. Now you know. Now you walk in it.

Welcome to your treasure season. This is your time to shine like the gold you've always been. Your vessel might have a few cracks, but that's what makes the light of God shine through even brighter. Those cracks aren't flaws—they're proof of restoration.

You are a treasure, valuable, chosen, and divinely crafted. Never forget it. Never settle for less. Never apologize for knowing your worth. Live every day like the treasure you are, and let the world see what God's glory looks like when it shines through you.

You are not disposable. You are not a mistake. You are the masterpiece of a God who sees worth in every single piece of you even the ones that were broken. And when He restores, He doesn't glue the fragments together hoping they'll hold. He transforms them into something stronger, more radiant, and more beautiful than before.

So lift your head. Reclaim your value. Walk like royalty. Speak like someone who carries heaven's DNA—because you do.

This is your treasure season. And it's time for the world to see you shine.

Chapter 9

"It's a New Dawn: Your Season of Refreshing

Dawn always comes. Always. No matter how long the night, no matter how dark the darkness, no matter how cold the hours before sunrise, dawn always comes. And when it does, it doesn't ask the night for permission. It doesn't negotiate with the darkness. It simply arrives and changes everything.

Your dawn is here. Your new day is breaking. We've walked through a lot together in these pages. We've taken off grave clothes that had become too comfortable. We've identified and disconnected from spiritual freeloaders and seed droppers. We've survived being pressed but not crushed. We've reclaimed our identity as treasures, not trash. We've seen God restore what was broken and give double for our trouble. Now it's time to walk into the new dawn He's been preparing while you were surviving your night.

Psalm 30:5 declares, "Weeping may endure for a night, but joy comes in the morning." Notice it doesn't say joy might come. It says joy comes. It's not a possibility; it's a promise. Your weeping has endured long enough. Your morning is here.

Refreshing comes when you return to the presence of God. True renewal doesn't come from another vacation or a temporary distraction; it comes from His Spirit reviving your soul.

In your new dawn, God is refreshing your mind with peace that silences anxiety. He's refreshing your spirit with hope that refuses to quit. He's refreshing your heart with joy that outlasts sorrow.

David knew this kind of refreshing when he said in Psalm 23:3, *"He restores my soul."* Restoration means God doesn't just fix what's broken—He breathes new life into what was once lifeless.

Think of Elijah. After calling down fire from heaven, he collapsed under a juniper tree, ready to give up. But God sent an angel to wake him and feed him, saying, "The journey is too much for you." After rest and nourishment, Elijah rose with renewed strength. That's refreshing. It's God reviving what exhaustion tried to kill.

Your new dawn isn't just for you. Isaiah 60:1-3 declares, "Arise, shine; for your light has come! And the glory of the Lord is risen upon you. For behold, the darkness shall cover the earth, and deep darkness the people; but the Lord will arise over you, and His glory will be seen upon you. The Gentiles shall come to your light, and kings to the brightness of your rising."

People still in their night need to see your dawn. They need to know morning is possible. They need to see someone who survived the darkness and made it to daylight. Your new dawn is someone else's hope that their night will end too.

This is why God allowed your night to be so long and so dark. The darker your night, the brighter your dawn. The longer your winter, the more glorious your spring. The deeper your valley, the higher your mountain.

Once dawn breaks, you have to protect it. The enemy would love to drag you back into night thinking. He would love to convince you that your dawn is temporary, that night is coming back, that this refreshing won't last.

Here's how to protect your dawn:

Stay in the Word. Psalm 119:105 says, "*Your word is a lamp to my feet and a light to my path.*" The Word keeps you in the light even when circumstances try to cast shadows.

Maintain your praise. Psalm 113:3 says, *"From the rising of the sun to its going down, the Lord's name is to be praised."* Praise maintains your dawn atmosphere. It keeps you in the light of His presence.

Guard your associations. Second Corinthians 6:14 warns, *"What fellowship has light with darkness?"* Don't let people who are committed to their night steal your dawn. Don't let those who prefer darkness dim your light.

Rise up, survivor. Rise up, overcomer. Rise up, warrior. Your dawn has come.

Walk into it with confidence. You've earned this moment. You survived the night. You endured the darkness. You weathered the storm. You outlasted the attack. You persevered through the pain.

Now receive your reward. Receive your refreshing. Receive your restoration. Receive your new day.

The same God who kept you through the night has brought you into the dawn. The same grace that sustained you in darkness will establish you in light. The same power that preserved you in the valley will now promote you on the mountain.

This is not the end. It's the beginning. The past has passed. The storm has settled. The pressing, the pruning, and the pain have all produced purpose. God is saying, *"Arise, shine, for your light has come"* (Isaiah 60:1).

The night is over. The shadows have lifted. The sun of His glory is rising over your life.

You have survived enough winters. This is your spring. You have cried enough tears. This is your laughter. You have endured enough loss. This is your harvest.

So lift your head. Wipe your eyes. Breathe deeply. The season has shifted. The atmosphere has changed. The light of a new dawn is breaking through. You are walking into your season of refreshing.

Your season of refreshing isn't coming here. Your new dawn isn't approaching; it has arrived. Your new day isn't on the horizon; it's happening right now.

The night is over. The grave clothes are gone. The weight of the past has lifted. What was broken is now restored. What was labeled as trash has been revealed as treasure. What the enemy meant for harm has turned into a double portion blessing.

Now walk boldly in your dawn. Live freely in your light. Flourish in your refreshing.

Your story of brokenness has become your story of wholeness. Your testimony of survival has become your testimony of revival. What was once a journey through darkness has become a journey into light.

It's a new dawn and it's yours. Arise and shine. Your light has come.

The journey from brokenness to wholeness is complete. But your journey in wholeness? That's just beginning.

Welcome to your new dawn.
Welcome to the rest of your life.

A CALL TO THE KINGS

Brothers, this moment is for you.

For too long, men have carried weight that nobody acknowledged, fought silent battles that nobody saw, and pushed through seasons that would have crushed someone less resilient. You have been expected to lead without ever being taught, to be strong without ever being supported, and to keep going even when your soul was tired. Yet here you stand. Still breathing. Still fighting. Still trying to become the man God had in mind when He formed you.

But before you rise into your next level, there is a warning every man must hear in love.

Do not become an Er-type man.

In the manuscript, Er represents a man who was present but not participating. He had position but not purpose. He watched but never engaged. He enjoyed the benefits of connection but refused the responsibility that came with it. Er was a man who stood in the right place but carried the wrong posture.

And God is calling you to be more than that.

An Er-type man is physically available but emotionally absent.
He wants partnership without contribution.
He wants respect without responsibility.
He wants fruit without planting anything.
He wants destiny without discipline.

Brothers, that is not who you are. A king does not watch life. A king builds it. A king does not drop seed. A king protects it. A king does not sit on the sidelines. A king stands in his assignment.

God created you to cultivate, to lead, to shape, to cover, and to carry His power with honor. There is treasure inside you. There is authority inside you. There is spiritual weight inside you that hell recognizes, and heaven expects you to use. You were designed to walk in strength, not silence. You were created to rise, not retreat.

Many men cope through shutting down or pushing people away. Some carry wounds from childhood, failed relationships, disappointment, rejection, or shame. But healing is not humiliation. Healing is holy. Healing is strength. Healing is how you show God that you refuse to be an Er-type man, wasting your life by hiding from what hurt you.

Real strength is not pretending you never broke. Real strength is letting God make you whole.

Brothers, this is your call to rise as kings.

You are not just survivors. You are conquerors. Scripture tells us that we are more than conquerors through Christ. You were not created to barely get by or simply cope through life. You were created to take authority, to win spiritual battles, to break cycles, to set order in your home, to protect your purpose, and to walk with a boldness that comes from knowing who your Father is.

Your season is shifting. The same way God raised up David from the fields, He is raising you. The same way He strengthened Joshua to lead, He is strengthening you. The same way He took ordinary men and gave them extraordinary power, He is placing that same power inside your spirit.

Do not underestimate the weight you carry. Do not downplay the anointing on your life. Do not silence your voice because life tried to break it. You have authority that angels respect. You have resilience that storms cannot drown. You have influence that shifts atmospheres.

And that is why you must refuse to be an Er-type man.
Er lost his blessing because he refused to grow.
Er forfeited his calling because he would not participate.
Er missed destiny because he never matured.

But you are stepping into a different story. You are becoming a man who shows up with intention. You are becoming a man who leads with wisdom. You are becoming a man who invests in what matters. You are becoming a man who loves on purpose. You are becoming a man whose presence brings stability, peace, and strength.

You are becoming the kind of man whose family feels safe when you speak.
You are becoming the kind of man whose prayers carry power.
You are becoming the kind of man who refuses to drop the seed God trusted you with.
You are becoming the kind of man who builds legacy while others waste time.

A king is not perfect. A king is growing. A king is accountable. A king is teachable. A king is intentional. A king is willing to confront himself so he can lead others well.

Brothers, God is calling you into your kingship.

Rise with courage.

Rise with clarity.

Rise with wholeness.

Rise with authority.

You are needed.

You are valued.

You are chosen.

You are powerful.

You are evolving into the man God designed you to be.

And as you rise into your royal place, heaven stands behind you.

The Epilogue

We spend so much time trying to qualify ourselves. Trying to be good enough, smart enough, holy enough, healed enough, whole enough to be used by God. We create these elaborate checklists of what we need to accomplish before we're qualified for purpose. But what if I told you that you already have the only qualification that matters?

You're still here.

You're still breathing. Still standing. Still reading. Still believing enough to make it to the last page of this book. That's not an accident. That's not luck. That's divine preservation for divine purpose.

Revelation 12:11 says, "And they overcame him by the blood of the Lamb and by the word of their testimony, and they did not love their lives to the death." Your testimony isn't what's going to qualify you someday. Your testimony has already qualified you today. The fact that you have a testimony means you survived something. And your survival is your qualification.

Every Scar Tells a Story

Jesus knew something about scars that we're just beginning to understand. After His resurrection, when He appeared to His disciples, He didn't hide His scars. He displayed them. In John 20:27, He told Thomas, "Reach your finger here, and look at My hands; and reach your hand here, and put it into My side."

The resurrected Christ still had scars. Think about that. The glorified body of Jesus, the body that could walk through walls, which could appear and disappear, that had conquered death itself, still bore scars. Why? Because scars tell stories that words never could. Scars provide proof that wounds can heal. Scars demonstrate that what tried to kill you didn't succeed.

Your scars aren't disqualifications. They're credentials. That scar from the divorce? That's your degree in surviving rejection. That scar from the abuse? That's your certification in overcoming trauma. That scar from the addiction? That's your qualification to speak to others in bondage. That scar from the loss? That's your authority to comfort those who mourn.

Stop trying to hide your scars. Stop being ashamed of them. Stop seeing them as evidence of failure. They're evidence of survival. They're proof of God's keeping power. They're your qualification for ministry.

Let's do some math. According to statistics, you shouldn't be here. The odds of you being born were about 1 in 400 trillion. Then add all the times you could have died but didn't. The accidents that almost happened. The diseases that could have taken you. The despair that almost won. The attacks that almost succeeded.

Yet here you are. Still alive. Still breathing. Still standing.

Jeremiah 1:5 declares, "Before I formed you in the womb I knew you; before you were born I sanctified you; I ordained you a prophet to the nations." Before you took your first breath, God had already qualified you. Your survival isn't luck. It's purpose.

Every time you survived something that should have destroyed you, God was saying, "Not yet. I'm not done with them. They have work to do. They have lives to touch. They have testimonies to share. They have breakthroughs to birth."

Your Testimony Is Someone Else's Breakthrough

Here's what you need to understand about your survival story: it's not just yours. Your testimony is community property in the Kingdom of God. Your breakthrough is someone else's blueprint. Your survival is someone else's hope.

Right now, someone is going through what you went through. They're in the pit you climbed out of. They're fighting the battle you won. They're facing the giant you defeated. They're wearing the grave clothes you took off. They're in the night you survived to see dawn.

They need to know it's survivable. They need to see someone who made it through. They need to hear someone say, "I've been where you are, and there's another side to this valley."

Your survival qualifies you to speak to their situation. You don't need a degree in counseling to say, "I survived that, and so can you." You don't need ordination papers to say, "God brought me through, and He'll bring you through too." You don't need anyone's permission to share what God has done in your life. Your healing will become their hope. Your survival will become their strategy. Your breakthrough will become their blueprint.

So keep shining your light. Keep telling your story. Keep walking in purpose.

The Qualification That Can't Be Revoked

Here's the beautiful thing about being qualified by survival: no one can revoke this qualification. They can question your education, but they can't question your experience. They can debate your theology, but they can't deny your testimony. They can critique your methods, but they can't cancel your miracles.

When the enemy tries to disqualify you by bringing up your past, remind him that your past is exactly what qualifies you. When people try to silence you by pointing out your imperfections, remind them that perfect people can't minister to imperfect situations.

Jesus chose fishermen, tax collectors, zealots, and former prostitutes to change the world. He chose people with stories, with scars, with testimonies of transformation. He's still choosing the same kind of people today. He's choosing you.

Your Survival Assignment

As you close this book and step into your new dawn, your season of refreshing, your time of restoration, remember that your survival comes with an assignment:

Live out loud. Don't hide your story. Don't minimize your testimony. Don't whisper when you should shout. Someone needs to hear that survival is possible.

Love the broken. You know what broken feels like. You know what rejection feels like. You know what despair feels like. Use that knowledge to love others through their breaking.

Lead from your scars. Your scars give you authority to speak to certain situations. Don't lead from your perfection, lead from your healing. Don't minister from your strength; minister from His strength perfected in your weakness.

The Final Declaration

Stand up one last time. This is your commissioning. This is your sending. This is your qualification ceremony:

"I qualify because I'm still alive. Every breath I take is proof that God isn't finished with me. Every scar I bear is evidence of God's healing power. Every test I've survived has become my testimony.

I am not disqualified by my failures. I am qualified by my survival. I am not limited by my past. I am not defined by what I've been through. I am refined by what I've been through.

God kept me alive for a reason. My survival has a purpose. My story has an assignment. My scars have a ministry. My testimony has a destination.

I will not be silent about what God has done. I will not hide what He has healed. I will not minimize what He has maximized. I will not whisper what He wants me to shout.

I am qualified. I am commissioned. I am sent. I am ready.

Because I'm still alive, and that's all the qualification I need."

Your Commencement

This isn't the end. This is your commencement. You've graduated from brokenness to wholeness. You've completed the course from victim to victor. You've finished the journey from barely surviving to thriving.

But graduation isn't the end of learning; it's the beginning of applying what you've learned. Your survival has qualified you for a ministry you might not even know exists yet. Your scars have prepared you for people you haven't even met yet. Your testimony is the key to doors that haven't even appeared yet.

Walk in your qualification. Own your survival. Celebrate your scars. Share your story. Live your testimony.

The world is waiting for what your survival has qualified you to deliver. Heaven is cheering for what your breakthrough is about to birth. Hell is trembling at what your testimony is about to destroy.

You qualify because you're still alive.

Now go live like it.

Go love like it.

Go lead like it.

Your survival is your qualification. Your qualification is someone else's salvation.

Your story isn't over. In fact, it's just beginning.

"And they overcame... by the word of their testimony."
- Revelation 12:11

You are that testimony.

You are that overcomer.

You are qualified.

Now go change the world with your survival story.

www.ingramcontent.com/pod-product-compliance
Lightning Source LLC
Chambersburg PA
CBHW032048090426
42744CB00004B/123